Michael Green is a journalist. He has worked for the Press Association and *The Times*. Since 1960 he has been with the *Daily Telegraph*, as a home reporter, in Africa and the USA. He was deputy news editor 1973–79 and since then has edited the 'Peterborough' column which is the newspaper's tailpiece.

Also by Michael Green in Sphere Books:

THE PETERBOROUGH BOOK
TONIGHT JOSEPHINE

The Daily Telegraph

The Peterborough Book II

**Selected and compiled by
MICHAEL GREEN**

SPHERE BOOKS LIMITED
London and Sydney

First published in Great Britain by
David & Charles (Publishers) Ltd 1982
Copyright © *The Daily Telegraph* 1982
Published by Sphere Books Ltd 1984
30–32 Gray's Inn Road, London WC1X 8JL

TRADE
MARK

Set in Baskerville

Printed and bound in Great Britain by
Cox & Wyman Ltd, Reading

Introduction

On a BBC overseas service programme a few months ago an interviewer asked me one of those impossible general questions: 'Where exactly does "Peterborough" fit in the framework of *The Daily Telegraph*?'

I had to say that I often saw it as an antidote to the rest of the newspaper!

It is, alas, the fact that bad news makes news; so-called 'good news' papers have been tried and have all failed miserably. That doesn't mean to say that a newspaper has to be *all* bad: the *Telegraph* with its huge coverage across the world reports many cheerful items.

Only the column signed 'Peterborough', however, is guaranteed to be there every day as a sort of respite, even a sanctuary, from the inhumanity and sheer awfulness of so many of today's happenings. Of course, many a serious topic is aired, but the one unbreakable rule is that nothing but a printer's dispute shall prevent the appearance of a tail-piece paragraph devoted to raising a smile even on the grimmest day.

I can't hope to amuse all the people all of the time. I have been accused of many simple things from bad grammar to bad taste. Once I wrote a story of a ten-year-old boy who was taken to a coffee morning somewhere in Surrey which, it was explained to him, was in aid of the Save the Children Fund. 'Why?' he asked, 'Are they becoming extinct?' The next day I received a most touching letter pleading that I should not make fun of something so serious as this Fund.

Fortunately, most readers enter into the spirit of things. Just as important to me is the fact that they continue, despite the efforts of the Post Office to price any sort of social correspondence out of the household budget, to take the time and buy the stamps to send me likely tales.

To them, my eternal gratitude. May they long continue to take part in the hunt for the human side to these mechanical and threatening times.

The first book of 'Peterborough' tailpieces, leavened with some humorous items from mid-column, proved very popular when published in 1980. This second edition, taken mainly from the last four or five years, has been created on similar lines. The same technique of editing has also been used with the aim of cutting out repetitive phrases and, for example, references which would require explanatory footnotes. Such small reshuffling as has been necessary in no way changes the overall style, feeling and – I hope! – humour of the original.

Michael Green, 1982

Tourist Tales

Cock-a-doodle done
English holidaymakers arriving at their hotel in Crete
saw this comment in the visitors' book: 'Shoot that
cockerel! We don't wish to be awakened at dawn while
on holiday!'

Going in to dinner soon afterwards they were a little
alarmed to see high on the menu: 'Rouster in Whine
Sauce.'

Alo-ha!
A colleague just back from Hawaii swears that he saw
this advertisement: 'You will never find better or more
exciting bikinis than ours – they are simply the tops!'

Miracle holiday
One of Thomas Cook's holiday brochures offers this
attraction in Ibiza: 'The amenities of Santa Eulalia are a
fifteen-minute walk away, with a man-made beach just
five minutes walk across the river from the hotel.'

English tourists in France during this latest cross-Channel brouhaha about Common Market food prices may perhaps hesitate to accept the offer on one menu reported by a recently returned Eastbourne reader: 'Carafe d'eau du patron gratuite.'

A touch of Eastern...
An Aylesbury reader kindly supplied me with these excerpts from a menu in a Baghdad restaurant:

> Pimps No 1 or Pimps No 2
> Shrimps catstails
> Escalope Gordon Blue
> Cram Chaps
> Chauteaubriani for 3 parsons

Rhode Island Red
An American at breakfast at the Bay Tree Hotel, Burford, this week, was asked how he would like his boiled egg and replied: 'Please may I have it medium rare?'

On the coffee shop menu of the excellent Rincombe Hotel in Chiang Mai, northern Thailand, a recent tourist noted: 'Today's Special: Fried crispy wanton with beef and vegetables.'

Naturally
Notice outside a Hampshire village hall: 'Sports Club meeting, Thursday 7 pm. Speaker Mr – on Winter Holidays in Switzerland (with slides).'

Warm welcome
An English visitor to Gibraltar was comforted to see that directly opposite her bedroom was a door marked 'Fire Escape'. When she looked more closely she saw it was also marked 'Staff Only'.

Promises, promises
A reader touring in Scotland saw this sign in a village window: 'Bed & Breakfast with Local Honey.'

During a conducted tour of Caernarvon Castle the other day, an American tourist was heard to remark: 'It sure is a splendid place, but isn't it a pity they had to build it so near the railroad?'

Mayday, heyday!
This emergency notice is displayed in a small hotel in the Dordogne: 'In the event of fire, the visitor, avoiding haste, is to walk down the corridor and warm the chambermaid.'

There's a difference?
A poster near the harbour at Abersoch, North Wales, reads: 'Boats for hire – for fishing or pleasure.'

A Glastonbury reader reports sighting four American women downing their snack lunch at the George and Pilgrim before boarding their coach. 'No,' said one of them, 'I'm staying right here to do my postcards. You three go off round the town and tell me about it after. Where are we, anyway?'

Unladylike
Card seen on a packaged currant cake in a shop window near Hanover: 'English "Lady Cake" – Plum Cake mit Whisky.'

O'Really?
Seen on a stall at San Remo market, Italy, was a woollen pullover with the label: 'Best Scottish knitwear. Jock McPhoney. Made in Scotland.'

Tango thermidor
A traveller just back from Canada's Thousand Islands' area reports this notice: Restaurant
Live Lobsters
Dancing Nightly

Puss in boots
A Berkshire reader tells me that when her neighbour was going on holiday she asked: 'Would you be kind enough to feed the cat – so long as it doesn't put you out.'

Holiday relief
From an advertisement for a Florida holiday: 'Sun and snooze after a luscious gourmet lunch. Then climb on to the high board and dive into our king-size pool. We fill it with water every day.'

Miraculous journey
That tourists still think London a wonderful place was

confirmed for one 'local' this week when an American asked to be directed to Marvel Arch.

Right lines
Travellers in China can vouch for the enormous job the country faces in trying to modernise. A peasant in a remote part of Szechwan province asked a visitor if he had ever seen a train.

Was it true that a train was bigger than a house? Was it painted black as people said, and did it really belch smoke and travel great distances in a day? All true, said the visitor.

'One last question,' said the peasant. 'How many legs does it have?'

On Report

That boy!
Many thanks to the many parents who have volunteered
extracts from school reports. One teacher's comment, at
least, is a classic: 'The dawn of legibility in (this boy's)
handwriting discloses his utter inability to spell.'

From Devon comes the despairing: 'Adipose and
comatose.'

From Surrey, a masterpiece of bafflement: 'He seems
to float around the place with an air of discreet
flamboyance.'

A lady from Norfolk admits that when she was 9 years
old she was admonished with: 'If Josephine worked as
hard as she talks she would be our most brilliant pupil.'

Sadly, a mother recalls her son's description by his
headmaster: 'This boy will make a good foreman
judging by the way he watches other people work.' Not
very prescient, for the boy was killed on an RAF
wartime mission, aged only 19.

Comprehensively put
Another school report from yesteryear: 'This boy listens
in school with the flawless dignity of the dead.'

A Hampshire reader insists that under Headmaster's Comments in her nine-year-old son's report are the words: 'Unimaginative but reliable. Would make a good parent.'

More of a whimper

Hardly a bang of a report from the housemaster who wrote: 'Not a very good set of reports, but don't take too much notice of them – two of them, I know, were written by tired men.'

Reporting faithfully

John Timpson seized his moment on BBC radio's 'Today' programme to bemoan the apparent halt to my school report notes, and told of the metalwork pupil who 'if you give him the job, will finish the tools'.

My readers have, however, been as busy as ever, rediscovering such gems as:

'Tim's cheerful smile will get him through most things in life but not, I fear, the O Level Maths exam.'

'This boy is not only off the rails but half-way down the embankment as well.'

'His mind is like unto a muddy pond in which occasionally gleams a goldfish.'

A look at the other side of the school report scene is afforded by this contribution, just arrived on my desk: 'Rachel will have to work hard next term if she is to be sure of a GCE in June. A lot of his mistakes are due to carelessness.'

Country Life

Hallelujah!
From a Wirral, Cheshire, newspaper: 'On Wednesday... the William Morris Dancers will perform Handel's "Messiah".'

Smashing time
A Salisbury local newspaper's 'Entertainments' column includes for tomorrow the Western Area Planning Sub-committee, meeting in the municipal offices. Open every day is the Bottle Bank in Brown Street car park.

Crusty
A collecting box in an elaborate stone pillar in Blakeney, Norfolk, has a notice on it: 'Please help feed ducks.' Unfortunately, too many visitors have taken this request literally, so a new notice has had to be added next to the slot for the money: 'Do not stuff bread in here.'

Farnham Maltings Association newsletter reports that

*today there will be a big tidy-up-for-winter morning . . .
'when the small band of lady volunteer gardeners, who
work ceaselessly throughout the year, will get together
to sort the gardens out for the Spring. Please, would you
like to share a bed with someone? . . . Just turn up on the
15th.'*

And for second prize . . .
While on holiday in Torquay, a Bristol couple went to a
cabaret at the Rainbow House hotel. During the
evening they took part in a competition, which they
won.

Presenting them with a bottle of champagne, the
compere-comedian, Mike Swan, announced: 'You have
also won a free week's holiday . . . at our new hotel in
Vietnam. It's five star and you can see three of them
through the roof.'

Norman King, manager of the hotel, has now
received a solicitor's letter from Bristol demanding that
he honour the promise.

Hornrimmed spectacle
Squatters in Suffolk are having a thin time of it, thanks
to the growing popularity of a Sotterley farmer's
eviction technique. Around a cottage full of squatters
he erected a stout fence – and then put a bull inside.

Making the fur fly
Among the activities offered to prospective young
Conservatives at Chandler's Ford, Hampshire, are:
'Quizzes, debates, tenpin bowling and visits to such
places as Radio Solent and a minx farm.'

Really!
The gardens at Compton Acres, Poole, are also famous for their statues collected from all over the world. Admiring a group of beautiful bronzes a recent visitor was heard to utter this highest praise: 'They look so real! They could be made of plastic!'

Weather note: I see from the latest report on the Whitbread village cricket championship that when the captains of Canon Frome (Hereford) and Colwall (Worcs) went out for the toss the coin came down on its edge and stuck upright in the mud.

Working together
Back in the days of manual telephone exchanges, the operator in a little Midlands town used to get a call every day from a man who wanted to check the time. She found that an easy question, so I read in a Nottingham Methodist church magazine.

All she had to do was glance out of the window and she could see the clock on the local factory tower. Eventually, he explained to her why he made his daily call. 'You know the clock on the factory tower,' he said. 'Well, I have to see it keeps the correct time.'

An advertisement in the Westmorland Gazette *to which I can add no comment of any weight: 'CRUISE on Lake Windermere WITH CYRIL SMITH. Book your tickets now, space is limited.'*

Cumbrian fleshpots
A variation on an old notice, seen in a launderette in Kendal, Cumbria: 'Why don't you leave your clothes here and go out and enjoy yourselves.'

Old-fashioned service
Sign on the door of a Wiltshire village shop: 'Closed for lunch unless you want something.'

High note of the year
From the magazine of the Motor Caravanners Club: 'Regretfully, a favourite village hall used by Surrey members especially for barn dancing, the large one at Bletchingley, will not be available to us this autumn. Sudden wall cracks have appeared after our community singing last December and the future of the hall is in doubt...'

Arithmetic lesson
In a bookshop near Eton College there is a pile of illustrated books marked 'one shilling and sixpence'. A reader queried the price, to be told: 'One shilling and sixpence – that's seven and a half pence, sir.'

That's real comfort
An advertisement in the *Mid-Sussex Times* offers a £70,000 house at Clayton with '5 bedrooms, garage and car port, nine acres of woodland, including carpets'.

Easy does it
It is good to see that the leisured pace of country life goes on. The Ringwood & Fordingbridge (Hants) *Journal* reports that, prompted by a forest fire that threatened West Moors in 1976, a parish council emergency committee to deal with any crisis is 'now starting to take shape' and should meet in the autumn of 1980.

Real old soldiers
From the *Stratford-upon-Avon Herald*: 'The Royal British Legion took forty-five men and their widows on their annual outing, a tour of the Cotswolds...'

I have it from the vicar of a Northamptonshire village church that during a Christian unity meeting a list of local organisations was being drawn up. Suddenly a man's voice intervened: 'It's no use contacting the Young Wives in our village. They've disbanded and joined the Over-Sixties.'

Reaping rewards
A new members' meeting of Blandford Young Farmers Club at the Crown Hotel promises to be a lively affair. Their advertisement in the *Western Gazette* is headed: 'WAKE UP WITH A YOUNG FARMER!!!'

Up to par
From a report of the annual general meeting of a Lancashire golf club: 'The Secretary announced that, as in previous years, there would be a Christmas Eve

dinner dance. After discussion, it was agreed to hold it on Monday, December 24.'

Robin himself
A small boat tied up on the Deben, Woodbridge, Suffolk, has a notice: 'For sale £95. Bird nesting in locker, sale deferred until further notice.'

Put It This Way

Too true
From 'Travelling in Britain', a booklet issued by a New York travel agency: 'British Railways are used by all classes of the community. If you stand and watch commuters arriving at any of the London termini you will see for yourself that they are a cross section of the population.'

A woman was overheard to say at a buffet reception: 'I hate this lap-hazard way of eating.'

No four letter words
'Cheap' has become 'cost effective' in the world of the new businessman-bureaucrat and 'cheap at the price' has become the snappy catch-phrase: 'To service the user at the lowest possible cost under current environmental circumstances.' But surely the prize goes to the Ferranti official who speaks of an 'aerially delivered area denial system'. He means a bomb.

Lord Home has just offered a nice classroom definition of a Life Peer: 'A Lord who doesn't pass on when he dies.'

Minimum minions
A sign in the rear window of a car seen in Westminster declared: 'Cut Public Spending. Let's see the MINI in Ministries.'

Shocking state
An estate agent in Cornwall is offering: 'A character terrace cottage having terrified charm and great potential.'

A reader swears he heard an ITN reporter say of Sunday's mass jog in Hyde Park: 'The runners were broken down by age and sex.'

Book match
For some time the slogan 'Valerie is bonkers' has been seen on a Sussex youth club wall. It has now been joined by 'Ruth is stranger than fiction.'

Many A Slip

Going for a ride
As chairman of Burmah, sixty-six-year-old Sir Alastair Down is well aware of how competitive the oil industry can be. Even he was unnerved on a recent business trip to New York. Printed on top of the official programme for his visit was: 'Car – for the disposal of the chairman.'

A guerrilla band of Scunthorpe steel strikers was asked to picket Immingham Docks on the Humber. They arrived in the early hours before some big iron gates and set up their cordon insanitaire of placards and braziers. Only when dawn came did they realise they were in the wrong place. The gates led into a cemetery.

Away loss
I hear that Oldham Athletic Football Club is to lodge a protest with British Rail about a train that left on time.

As players and officials arrived at Euston last Saturday after their game with Chelsea they saw their soccer special pulling away. Oldham secretary Tom Finn commented: 'We shall be asking for some form of compensation. I have never known a special train set off exactly on time.'

Angus Maude, Paymaster-General, reports that on May 1, 1979, his department employed 869 civil servants and that on December 31 the pay roll was 896½. Has there been, his critics ask, a new definition of Whitehall staff cuts they haven't been told about?

Geography lessons
A reader was rather startled to read a Wedgwood blurb about painter Mary Vickers, which described her as 'born and raised in the small English village of Dagenham'. (To get there, observed a colleague, cross the Ford.)

There is more excuse for the confusion in an American magazine which identifies 'Newport, a town on the Isle of Wight in a part of Great Britain once referred to as Monmouthshire'.

An RAF Association plaque for 'services rendered' has been presented to retiring East Kent Times *editor, Fred Seymour. A generous gesture, indeed! In the last war he served with the only British anti-aircraft battalion that admitted shooting down an RAF plane.*

Dropping a brick
Sir George Young, Under-Secretary of State for Health, was most upset when he heard of the plight of one of his constituents in Acton. He wrote a long and sympathetic letter commencing: 'I am very sorry to learn of the

difficult conditions in which you and your family are living...'

A few days later the letter was returned by the Post Office. On the envelope was written: 'House demolished'.

According to the official newspaper produced by Maidstone Borough Council, the Mayor, Councillor Ernie Flood, declared: 'Waste in any form is something that no council should accept.' He had just sprayed what is described as 'a bottle of bubbly' all over the council's new bottle bank.

Ambition
Notice on the back of a tiny Fiat seen in Herefordshire: 'When I grow up I want to be a Cadillac.'

Missing letter
A reader who needed to make an urgent telephone call from a restaurant was mortified to find he did not have the number with him. 'No worry, sir,' said the Greek waiter, 'I get you directory. Which letter you want?'

'B, please,' my reader replied and waited for an anguished twenty minutes. Finally the waiter returned with all four volumes of the London directory, and a puzzled look. 'Sorry, sir, we have no letter B, only A, D, E, K, L, R, S or Z.'

Modern Times

Matter of principle
A Sussex reader reports facing this complaint from the mother of one of her son's schoolfellows: 'Four days in a row my son took a new pencil to school and your boy pinched every one of them. It's not the value of the pencils I'm concerned about,' she added. 'My husband gets all we need from the office.'

Good reception?
A newly married couple were seen to emerge from a local register office in Hampshire on Wednesday afternoon. The groom was listening (presumably to the Derby) on a transistor radio.

That figures
A garage mechanic was struggling to fit a new wing mirror. Eventually he gave up and was heard to mutter: 'It won't fit. It's one of those new universal fittings.'

American banks are making staff holidays compulsory. This is not in any spirit of benevolence, but because they have discovered that internal computer frauds most often come to light if the thieves are not always present to take care of the details.

Customary meal
The enduring British social scene was encapsulated in a Bristol branch office during a visit from headquarters. The manager looked into the office adjoining his own and was heard to say to its single occupant: 'I'm just off to lunch with the directors. You can go and have your dinner.'

Person to person
In the eyes of the Equal Opportunities Commission a housewife, according to a recent report, is now a non-employed-due-to-domestic-responsibilities person. In the eyes of employers, the Commission is just something to grin and bear, as two recent advertisements may testify:

'Attractive young ladies (m/f) required for respectable West End night club...'

'Tea person required. Ladies of either sex may apply...'

Crafty
An advertisement in the *Guardian* newspaper asks for a 'Craft Shop Organiser' for a project to do with the young unemployed. It stresses: 'We aim ... to develop a non-sexist approach to working with young people,' then adds: 'Applicants must be female...'

It was, I suppose, inevitable that the American pilot reported from New York yesterday to have had a sex change should then seek reinstatement from Eastern Airlines senior vice-president for operations.

Question of values
A reader in Ayrshire paid for a complex intravenous examination, a two-and-a-half hour operation with highly skilled staff using highly sophisticated equipment. It cost her £35.

Returning to her business, she had to call in a specialist firm to clear a blocked drain. That also took two-and-a-half hours, but cost £48.

Bang on
From the current price list of a San Francisco novelty store: 'Bring your kids up to date. Superb colour printed Globe of the World. Can be blown up in seconds.'

Overheard at Heathrow under the arrivals board of the UK inter-city flights to Manchester, Glasgow and Edinburgh: a young woman asked 'Where is Shuttle?'

One out, all ou...
Sign in the rear window of a car in Coventry: 'British Leyland is running out of wall to see the writing on.'

Steady job
News of the government's huge hand-out to preserve British Leyland was greeted by this shrewd analysis in

the *Oxford Mail*: it 'means that Cowley will build a new car this year and another one next year'.

Not a real nuisance yet

This conversation is reported from a Basingstoke housing estate: 'That lime tree in your front garden is an absolute menace. It hangs right down over the pavement.' The accused householder replied: 'I know. I can't imagine why the council don't order us to lop it.'

Below the belt

A woman passenger on a train travelling from Liverpool Street to Cambridge was overheard complaining to the guard that there was a terribly large gap under the toilet door. They ought, she declared, to put up a warning notice. 'What do you suggest?' he asked. 'Beware of limbo dancers?'

A reader who was recently in Fort Lauderdale, Florida, was told by a local journalist, with whom he had been discussing the rising tide of pornography, that the City Commission passed a strict law banning obscenity in books, magazines and records. Then it discovered that under the law its own wording was obscene and could not be published.

When is a souvenir...

T. W. Hendrick, honorary curator of Arundel Museum and Heritage Centre, was given notices by his local crime prevention officer stating in seven languages: 'You can be arrested for stealing.' He put one in each of the museum's eight galleries. They have all been stolen.

Art of tact
I hear from Legal and General that one of the pension schemes it devised recently for a client company met with stronger than usual opposition.

All the employees except one agreed voluntarily to join the scheme. The refusal of the one stubborn man reached a point when the managing director had no option but to call him in for a private word. 'If you don't sign,' he said, 'you're sacked.' There was only a vaguely visible blur as approval was put to paper.

'But tell me,' said the managing director, 'why did you hold out so long against the scheme?' Said the employee: 'Well, sir, no one really explained it to me quite as well as you.'

Normal working
A Swansea correspondent tried to contact a British Steel worker at a club he was known regularly to visit. He was told by the steward: 'John's working two-till-ten shift tonight, so he won't be in until eight.'

From Oslo comes the news that the National Congress of the Norwegian Pagan Society has decided in principle to operate a heathen Sunday school in the city. This would offer children of non-Christian families 'alternative constructive group activities.'

The higher fatuity
A teacher, asked by her headmaster to wear a skirt rather

than trousers 'in the interests of discipline and education' responded by asking if such a request had been addressed to her male colleagues.

Block of flats
A catalogue of properties to be sold by a west London auctioneer includes a block of flats in Muswell Hill. Offered with full vacant possession there is then a footnote: 'TO VIEW: By courtesy of the squatters.'

Threatened species
The conservationists are certainly getting their message across. A ten-year-old boy was taken to a coffee morning in a Surrey village which, it was explained, was in aid of the Save the Children Fund. 'Why?' he asked, 'Are they becoming extinct?'

Visiting his insurance broker, a Cornish reader found him occupied with a youth wanting to insure his motor cycle. Asked if he had any convictions, the boy shrugged and said 'only the usual'. This, it transpired, included fines for having no road fund licence, no insurance and an out-of-date driving licence – 'nothing to worry the insurance people,' he added.

Service ace?
A competitor in the Hotel Receptionist of the Year contest is described as 'qualified as a bi-lingual receptionist – she is fluent in sport'.

A Few Snacks

Generous tip
A memorable evening is promised at the Crown Inn at
Chiddingfold which announces: 'A chef is there to
barbecue T-bone steaks, beefburgers and sausages, with
customers giving a hand if they wish.'

Wine and tease
A business visitor to Sunderland searched the local
paper for the name of a good restaurant. All he could
find under the heading 'Food & Wines' was this:
'Organizer! Where can you get hot pies, mushy peas,
potato and gravy for only 48p...?'

Choice nuggets
A charity fund organiser who has been distributing
food parcels to pensioners in Battle, Sussex, reports: 'A
hundred-weight of coal was being delivered to people
who said they preferred it to food.'

*John Hunt, Conservative MP for Bromley Ravens-
bourne, confessed to the National Hairdressers' Feder-
ation meeting in Eastbourne that he was concerned*

about the town council's catering arrangements. He had been told that the sausages provided by the council were bought at a local shop which displayed the notice: 'All sausages made with the best conservatives.'

Delhicatessen
Written on a poster in a Birmingham doctor's waiting-room: 'Curry gives me indiagestion.'

Nomad rush
From the current notices of St John the Baptist church, Danbury, Essex: 'The Rev Andrew Adano, a nomad priest from North Kenya, will be coming to Danbury next Sunday for a week's stay at the Rectory. Anyone wishing to have him for a meal during his stay should ask the Rector, please.'

From an Ohio newspaper, extolling the lions of Longleat: 'They roam freely in the parkland, so if you see several of them approaching while you are sitting in your car, do not assume that they are preparing to charge. They are merely hoping for something to eat.'

Offal experience
A Shropshire newspaper reports: 'Established as Purveyors of Fine Meat over ninety years ago, the business will close at the end of the week ... At 6 pm on Saturday, Mr – will serve his last customer with a heavy heart.'

Chateau Liffey
Among the rows of seats reserved for officials and Press at this week's EEC meeting in Dublin Castle was a chair marked 'Cork Examiner'. A member of the French delegation peered at this and said, wonderingly: 'I never knew the Irish took wine so seriously'.

Try pacing about
A colleague asked a waiter in a Birmingham restaurant for an after-dinner cigar and was told: 'I'm sorry, sir, there are none. The chef went home early.' Astounded, he asked for the manager, who explained: 'We always keep the cigars locked up and only the chef has the key. His wife is expecting a baby tonight, so we let him off early.'

He added: 'They're too expensive to leave lying about.'

A visitor to the Olympic Games in Moscow returned to his hotel and said to one of the more amiable guides: 'Where is the nearest night club I can go for a meal?' She smiled and replied: 'Helsinki.'

From a Leeds University diary of events: 'Physiology Seminar – the value of a vagally innervated gastric antrum and intact pylorus in the surgery of peptic ulcer. Buffet afterwards.'

Home-made
A thirteen-year-old Kensington schoolboy who signs himself 'in favour of teacher retraining schemes' tells

me he recently spotted a mouth-watering dish being taken out of a dumb waiter at his school. 'Lovely,' he commented, 'it's quiche lorraine.'

'We'll have none of those foreign names here,' replied the proprietor's wife sternly. 'It's bacon and egg pie.'

Greedy
A holidaymaker just returned from Tunisia reports that the evening's delights offered by the hotel included 'snack charmer' and 'fire glutton'.

Mighty meaty
Item on the English language menu at an Istanbul restaurant: 'Mixed girrl and baked beings.'

According to John Doxat, who this week launched a handbook of cocktails and mixed drinks, a country's greatness is entirely relative to its degree of insobriety. Indeed, he argued, the British Empire was itself created by men 'who never drew a sober breath after the age of seven'.

Chip, chip, hooray!
Returning to solid English reality after a week of Christmas holiday feasting, here is an extract from the menu displayed in a cafe by Basingstoke bus station:
   Egg and Chips; Two Eggs and Chips; Egg Bacon and Chips; Two Eggs, Bacon and Chips; Sausage and Chips; Two Sausages and Chips; Bacon, Sausage and Chips; Egg, Sausage and Chips; Egg, Two Sausages and Chips; Two Eggs, Sausage and Chips; Two

Eggs, Two Sausages and Chips; Egg, Bacon, Sausage and Chips; Two Eggs, Bacon, Two Sausages and Chips; Egg, Bacon, Sausage, Beefburger and Chips...

It's good to be back!

Reasonable Answers

Suitable match
A flower arranger at a north London church was asked by the prospective bridegroom if she would decorate the church for his wedding. She agreed and asked what the colour scheme would be. He hesitated a moment, then said: 'Well, I'll be wearing a brown suit.'

Basic training
A form filled in by a girl applicant for a course in ballet at a West Midlands youth club began: 'Place and date of birth: Yardley, Jan 22, 1965.' It went on: 'Weight: 7 lbs 8 ozs. Height: about 12 inches.'

A question on a form issued by a Yorkshire local authority to its council house tenants asks for 'Length of Tenancy'. One resident replied: 'Approx. 38 feet.'

Woe there!
'Do you know how to stop a runaway horse?' demanded the lecturer at a Sussex club during a talk entitled:

'Coping with animals.'
   'Yes,' said a gruff voice. 'Bet on it.'

Lesson for us all
'What was the secret of your success?' asked the man from BBC TV of Reg White, our gold medal winning yachtsman from Brightlingsea. 'Well,' said Reg, 'we just kept in front all the time...'

A BBC reporter, interviewing some of the brave, handicapped young folk in the ten-mile 'race' at Derwentwater on Bank Holiday Monday asked: 'What was the worst part?' Without a pause, one girl said with feeling: 'The last four miles.'

Common entrance
A young Englishwoman, joining the staff of a London hotel, filled in the usual enrolment form. She put her date of birth, 27.5.1955, paused at the next column set aside for Common Market nationals which asks for date of entry into Britain and then wrote: 27.5.1955.

Important announcement
An elderly Lady Bracknell-like passenger turned to her fellow travellers on a Finchley Road bus after being addressed by the conductor as 'Ma' and declared: 'I do not recall giving birth to that man!'

Making her mark
'I'm not a customer here,' a teenage girl told a cashier in

a Cardiff bank, 'but could you change this money order for me? I'm the Miss – it's made payable to.' The cashier asked: 'Have you any means of identification?' The girl thought for a moment and then said hesitantly: 'Well, there's a mole on my right thigh.'

A colleague who dialled a wrong number the other day found himself speaking to a family planning clinic. To the lady who asked if she could help he rather sharply replied that his youngest child was now 17 years old. She offered him a refresher course.

Note taken
A notice in a Sussex club asks: 'Will any member volunteer to teach Pitman shorthand one evening a week?' To this someone has added: 'I thought he knew it.'

Piqued?
On a poster outside a Norfolk Hall advertising: 'Baldness: is there a cure?' someone has written: 'No, prepare to meet thy dome.'

Public Announcements

Styx and stones
Severn Trent water authority are already on record as addressing a letter to the 'Occupier, Public Convenience'. Now the Vicar of Burton Joyce with Bulcote, the Rev David Johnson, writes to say that the same outfit also tried to contact 'The Occupier, Cemetery, Church Road, Burton Joyce'. He resisted the temptation to return it marked 'no active occupier in residence'.

All animals are equal?
The current *Radio Times* has an interview about exams with John Mann, secretary of the Schools Council, which quotes him as saying: 'It is not very satisfactory to divide kids into sheep and goats...'

South Glamorgan Institute for Higher Education, Cardiff, is offering 'Degree in Dietetics (four-year Sandwich Course)'.

No small change

Another nice example of how local government spends its time and our money comes with a circular now doing the vast rounds of the Greater London Council. It states: 'As Miss Lee's official title is Controller of Transportation and Development, the Department's name has now been changed from Transport and Development to Transportation and Development Department.'

Increased output

Latest contributor to the ever-expanding dictionary of obfuscation is the Post Office Users National Council, who announced:

'A request to the Minister for additional staff resources even on a temporary basis, to allow us to achieve a more in-depth customer input into the formulation of Post Office policies, received a sympathetic hearing but a negative response.'

Translated: 'They wouldn't let us have any more staff.'

Bang to rights

Following a collision between a messenger and a jogger in a basement corridor, the Ministry of Defence has issued a request to all fitness enthusiasts 'not to run in the Old War Office corridors since fast moving objects are regarded as a hazard by the Health and Safety at Work Executive'.

Following that Bomb

The reaction of Japanese bureaucracy to major events –

'Ah, so?' – seems to be encapsulated in the recollection of a former prisoner of war who arrived in Thailand in 1945. On arrival in Bangkok, news that the war was over was confirmed by a Japanese NCO who climbed on to a railway wagon and announced that 'the Japanese emperor has graciously given peace to the world'.

It certainly is

Yes, it's hard to believe, says an advertisement for Hants & Dorset and Provincial buses, but if you go to your local bus station you can buy a half-fare Personpass.

Room at the top

An Environment Department circular listing the effects of the Budget proposals on local authorities contains the sentence: 'It is clear that a reduction in current expenditure must mean a reduction in jobs.' The brief document is signed by seven Under-Secretaries and one Assistant Under-Secretary.

No joke for sheep

The public relations departments of our county councils are not noted for their creative flair, but from Winchester I hear of a possible exception. A Hampshire council hand-out on the threat of sheep scab was headed: 'Mite Bite Might Blight Sheep.'

The hard way

South Eastern Electricity Board, in its latest apologia for rising prices, offers this helpful suggestion under the heading: If Hardship Hits You. 'If ... there is real hardship you can have a slot meter, but . . ., of course, a slot meter will cost you more each quarter.'

An amendment to the Hammersmith and Fulham District Plan approved by that council's planning policy committee states: 'Delete bottlenecks. Insert localised capacity deficiencies.'

Where else?
Page 116 of the index of the current standing orders of the House of Commons begins:
   Scottish Grand Committee
   Scottish Standing Committee
   Seats: see under Members

No kidding!
Under the heading 'Hairy Horrors on the March', the Tower Hamlets civic newspaper declares: 'Most household pests are easily recognisable . . . But for health reasons you should normally keep your distance, especially in the case of children.'

Kafka lives
A colleague who telephoned the visa department of the Czechoslovak embassy to ask about a visa never got a reply. He telephoned the consular department to ask why.

He was told that although the visa department was

open between 10 am and 1 pm the telephones were never answered because the Officials were 'too busy'. The telephones, it was explained, were answered only between 2 pm and 4 pm when the visa department was closed.

A 'Root and Branch survey' Working Party was set up at Southampton recently to report on ways of reducing and streamlining the university's committee structure. From the campus magazine 'Viewpoint' I learn that the working party has been unable to arrange a date for a meeting since all its members are fully occupied on other committees.

Taxing words

In its continuing effort to make its tax forms more intelligible, the American revenue service fed some sample words into the computer, which had been programmed to reject awkward ones. Among the words and terms the computer did not like were: spouse, deduction, taxpayer, social security and Internal Revenue Service.

Friends initially

A new word – 'posselcue' – has been officially adopted by the California State Census which wanted – please, don't ask me why – a term for their records more impersonal than wife, boy-friend or lover. Out of the depths of the bureaucratic mind sprang, full grown, the posselcue. Its definition: a Person of Opposite Sex Sharing Living Quarters, or POSSLQ.

Heated debate

Parish councillors in the village of Awsworth, Notts, are to ban smoking during their meetings. They find the room gets so smoky the fire alarm keeps going off.

Private Prattle

Tweety pies
An alert Kensington reader has drawn my attention to
what she regards as an awful American habit of adding
twee comments to simple newspaper birth announce-
ments and which seems to be catching on over here.
From recent columns of *The Daily Telegraph* she has
collected:
'A son to sort out Nichola and Emma...'
'A son – a partner in crime for...'
'A sparring partner for...'
'A nuisance for...'
'1st child to a very clever mother...'
'A cadet pair for Bisley...'
'A fourth for Bridge...'
'A co-pilot for...'
'Another member of the wrecking brigade...'
'That's my boy!'
However, as she says, it no doubt 'Keeps a lot of
couples very busy and happy'.

*In the 'Forthcoming Marriages' column of a West
Country newspaper I see that a marriage had been*

arranged between Miss M and Mr B which, 'all things being equal', should occur in March. 'Close friends have our permission to make a book on the likelihood of it actually taking place at all.'

Youthful auntie

A twelve-year-old girl's school essay on 'The Opposite Sex' is reported to have included the sentence: 'I do not think much of the opposite sex because when I want to do anything they want to do the opposite.'

Smile and a Prayer

Coming in on...
A Farnborough schoolteacher reports asking a seven-year-old boy during a religious education class: 'Why do we say "amen" at the end of our prayers?' After some thought, the boy replied: 'It's a special way of saying "over and out" to God.'

First things first
A Sunday school teacher in York talked on the subject of 'Repentance' for some time and, while summing up, asked her class what was the first essential before we could expect forgiveness. Came the reply: 'Please, Miss, we must sin.'

Any old carols?
Answering a knock at her door, a Bolton housewife discovered a small boy who asked her: 'Can we sing some carols for you, Missus?' Reasonably, she asked: 'We? I can only see one of you.' Replied the boy: 'Oh, no. I've got a friend. He's working the other side of the street.'

We three kings (reprise)

The other night in Biggleswade, a reader tells me, 'three small persons' sang carols, knocked on her door and enthused over the 15p she gave them. An hour later another three arrived, sang, knocked, and wished her a Merry Christmas for 20p – 'I had no more 5ps.'

A little later, yet another trio arrived, their shining faces somewhat familiar. Then, says my correspondent, 'it dawned. The little beasts had executed two quick changes of clothing.'

From a letter signed by your friend and Rector in the Cliffe and Cooling (Kent) parish newsletter: 'I am always particularly glad to hear of any cases of sickness, especially when they are long term.'

Relative merits

July's parish magazine of All Saints, Woodham, Surrey, prints the story of the vicar who had a company of gypsies camped in a field near his church. They moved on, leaving behind them a dead donkey.

When the vicar rang the local council, the official who answered, being something in the nature of a wag, replied that he understood it was the duty of the vicar to bury the dead. 'That may be so,' said the vicar, 'but I thought it was at least my duty to inform the relatives of the deceased.'

Lovely tip

An Ulverston reader saw a bishop, in gaiters and apron, in a restaurant, being asked by the waitress if he would sign the bill and let her keep it. He gladly did so and in episcopal style added a cross to his name. 'Oh, how sweet of you,' said the girl. 'And a kiss as well!'

A notice in a church in Phoenix, Arizona, states: 'Prayers have to be notified on the correct form or they will not be processed.'

Occasions for prayer

From the April newsletter of the parishes of Bessingby and Carnaby in east Yorkshire, not far from Hull:

April	23 Wednesday	St George, Patron Saint of England
	25 Friday	St Mark Evangelist
	27 Sunday	Easter 3
May	1 Thursday	SS Philip & James, Apostles & Martyrs
	3 Saturday	Rugby League Cup Final

I am indebted to the Ely Diocesan magazine Contact, *for discovering this local newspaper report: 'The sudden gust of wind took all who were at the ceremony by surprise. Hats were blown off and copies of the Vicar's speech and other rubbish were scattered over the site.'*

Love thy neighbour

Written on a poster in a Hampshire public library: 'Ecumenism means getting to know the opposite sects.'

Our Mediator
Overheard in Coventry between two business executive types: 'The way the Church of England is going we'll have to form a New Centre Church. They talk about unity and when they announce the Lord's Prayer you have to say "Which one?"'

Seven's veil
Overheard conversation: Boy aged 10: 'Do you believe in God?' – Girl aged 7: 'What will He do to me if I say "No?"'

Seize the time
From the parish magazine of Mortimer West End and Padworth, Berkshire: 'It appears the General Synod found the debate on "Sex" rather an embarrassing subject, which just goes to show how our elected members can so easily miss a chance to make the best of an opportunity.'

Conversation between two girls, aged 9 or so: 'I'm a virgin in our nativity play.' Scoffed the other: 'That's nothing, I'm an angel.' Declared the first, indignantly: 'It's much harder to be a virgin.'

Lack of faith?
A spiritualist church in Worthing has this ominous sign on its notice board: 'No healing during August.'

Inside job

From a west country parish's notices of the week: 'Wanted, One man (at least) to take a turn in cleaning the gents' loo off the Atrium. You do this at your own convenience.'

Bit out of date

During an afternoon rehearsal in Canterbury Cathedral last month of a singers' course organised by the Royal School of Church Music, an American tourist was heard to remark: 'Say, do they still hold services here?'

Stern morality

A Devon clergyman tells me he spent a night recently at an Exeter hotel and was invited to share a table at dinner with an unescorted lady to whom he had been introduced in the lounge. After a pleasant meal, the waitress asked: 'Would you like a pot of coffee?' But then she paused and after a moment's reflection declared: 'You've got separate room numbers. You shouldn't share a pot. I'll bring two cups.'

From the Mouths of...

Children

What else?
Conversation was about the flight of the American space shuttle and the four-year-old daughter, who had been listening in, was asked if she knew what space was. 'Yes,' she replied immediately, 'a place in the car park.'

Sounds like it
Pupils at a Shrewsbury school were asked for a definition of 'nostalgia'. One twelve-year-old wrote: 'It is Welsh for "Good-night".'

From a thirteen-year-old's essay: 'I don't like the Labour party because I think their a whole load of Communists. The Conservatives cut down on Public Spending and the Liberals aren't so brilliant either. Why not let the Queen have a go for a change?'

Room for improvement?

Quoted in a Jersey prep school's booklet, 'A Decade of Howlers': 'Please sir, what's this year's Nativity Play about, sir?'

Price rises bite

This note was found under the pillow of a Nottingham reader's little girl along with a newly shed baby tooth: 'Dear Fairies, Please may I have more money for my tooth as ivory is getting more expensive. Say about 10p more, will that do?'

Worldly wise

Judging by their answers to a recent general knowledge examination, the small boys of Haileybury Junior School have an impressive grasp on reality. A selection in the school magazine reveals a certain world-weariness, for instance, with politics:

Who is the Prime Minister? – The leader of the government. Who is the Deputy Prime Minister? – Woody Whitehorse. The Prime Minister denounced a Russian spy, name him. – Wedgewood Benn. Who wrote 'Bleak House'? – Dennis Healey. What have these three in common: Mr Callaghan, Mr Heath, Sir Harold Wilson? – Margaret Thatcher.

What is an apiarist? – A gorilla who plays the piano. Who designed the Dambusters' bouncing bomb? – Pinewood Studios. Which Robert learned from a spider? – Robert Muffet. What does VAT stand for? – Vast amount of tax.

An Oxfordshire reader tells me that the latest entry in her ten-year-old son's nature notebook reads: 'This morning a tiny blue tit who was eating from the bird table in the garden was nearly done for by a whopping great missile thrush.'

Ever hopeful

An enterprising ten-year-old was seen outside Farringdon Station, London, on November 18 still requesting – and receiving – pennies for the Guy. Asked if she was starting early for next year, she replied: 'No! I missed this year 'cos we were away.'

Catkin?

A four-year-old girl watched with fascination the Royal Tournament's team of RAF guard dogs go through their paces until the moment when they did their tightrope walk. She then declared: 'They could have got a cat to do that much more easily.'

Biblical question

From Farnham, Surrey, I hear of the twelve-year-old who is clearly taking her social studies seriously. She commented to her parents: 'It's just as well Jesus isn't living now. They'd never crucify him, just put him on probation for six months and that would have spoiled all his plans.'

Layman's language

Pupils at a Birmingham school were asked to translate

the saying: 'J'y suis, j'y reste.' One boy wrote: 'I am Swiss and I am having a lie down.'

Octo-jane-eyrian
It is reported from a Hampshire county library that an argument in the children's section was silenced by one aggressive girl who snapped: 'My grandmother has read Jane Eyre eight times!'

Sense of direction
Seeking to improve her young son's poor knowledge of geography, a Norfolk reader persuaded him to take up stamp collecting. Only two weeks later she had striking proof of how wise she had been. 'Where is Spain?' she asked him. Without hesitation he replied: 'Five pages after Portugal.'

A group of children from the Boys' and Girls' Welfare Society came from Cheshire to London and were given tea on the splendid Members' terrace of the House of Commons overlooking the Thames. 'What do you think of this?' asked a teacher. After thoughtfully looking around her and staring at her cup and saucer, a thirteen-year-old girl replied: 'The tea's a bit strong.'

Ship bored
What is 'wanderlust'? was a question put to senior girls at a Southend school. One girl replied: 'It is what people go on cruises for.'

Juicing it up

From deepest Gloucestershire I hear the sound of awful truth in a childish treble. 'My four-year-old grand-daughter', writes a correspondent, 'was duly impressed by the directions not to drink and drive. She said (somewhat smugly): "But we don't do that, do we, mummy? We stop, have a drink, and then drive on." The drink is orange juice, of course!'

Grown-ups

Medical report

To be charitable, let us say it was a Freudian slip when a Sussex teacher wrote on a pupil's report that his 'excuses are always interesting and varied. I am, however, running out of patients.'

V. promising

A friend who needed to find out the Shakespeare set plays for 1981–2 'A' Level syllabus, telephoned the Southern Universities Joint Board, where a voice at the other end of the line said: 'Well, it's Henry ... er, I'm not sure. It says one vee after it.'

Chips with nobody

From a Sussex school magazine: 'We wish him every happiness in his retirement. For over twenty-five years his learning and his wit have enriched the minds of all the boys to whom he taught English. It is true to say that as a teacher he was in a class by himself.'

Down in Devonshire there is a story of a boy in a motor car who asked his mother: 'What does a "one-in-five" sign mean at the top of hill?' Promptly she replied: 'It means there are only four more like it, dear.'

Fawlty order
A primary school in Wallingford, Oxon, sent a request to a local bookshop for a Diagnostic and Remedial Spelling Manuel and also a Teacher's Manuel.

Blighted troth
Under a poster advertising a talk to an Oxfordshire women's club on 'Alimony' someone has written 'The Bounty from the Mutiny'.

Highway code
A Wiltshire driving school owner tells me that when he took a woman pupil for her first lesson, she stuck a piece of paper on the driving wheel which said: 'Left is the side my wedding ring is on.'

Pas de scapegoat
Elizabeth Craven, writing in the International Dance Teachers Association magazine, reproduces some extracts from letters sent by parents to dance teachers, including this gem:

'Dear Miss –, If my darling Jessica May is in need of strictness from you, will you shout at the child next to her and that will be sufficient to upset her. Thank you for your co-operation.'

The Old Malthouse School has just produced a short history which includes some memories at random, such as that of the music master who said his favourite instrument was the viola because so few boys played it.

Aged relatively
Overheard from a visitor inspecting relics at Hatfield House: 'It says these stockings were worn by Queen Elizabeth.'

'I don't believe it,' returned her companion. 'They must mean her mother.'

Measure of distance
A passenger decanted at Gunnersbury Station in west London asked if it was far to Turnham Green which is, in fact, a mile away. 'Oh, it's quite a way,' came the reply. 'If you were going to walk you'd have to take a bus.'

A Touch of Menace

Caveat emptor
A sign seen in the window of a souvenir shop in Amman reads: 'Our boast – we never allow a dissatisfied customer to leave this store.'

Fair warning
Written in the dust under a 'Long Vehicle' sign on the back of a lorry seen in Winchester: 'But short temper.'

A notice in Nairobi's Snake Park: 'Trespassers will be poisoned.'

Time to switch off
Sign in a bar at a Norfolk inn: 'If you suddenly notice our colour TV don't drive. It's black and white.'

Flop house
An advertisement in the Buckingham *Advertiser* offers: 'Collapsible bed, ideal for guests...'

53

Monstrous regiments?
A notice in Yapton and Ford (Sussex) parish magazine
says that at the next meeting in the vicarage of the
Young Wives group 'there will be a demonstration of
war games'. And on to my desk drops a page from the
Sydney, Australia, YWCA centenary magazine which
announces: 'Discussion groups are being held on the
Third World War – beginning 14th July.' I think you
ladies are tipping your hand a bit early!

House trained, I hope
In the situations vacant column of the Kent and Sussex
Courier: 'Family help wanted, twin boys 4 years and
other animals...'

*A reader who went to pay his rates at Chiswick Town
Hall was not sure whether to be surprised or not at the
large notice outside the door saying: 'Blood donors this
way.'*

Overrule of the road
A sign attached to the back of a juggernaut lorry in
Southampton declared: 'Keep clear. I have the right of
weight.'

I arrest chew
Sign seen outside a house in Clacton: 'Doberman
Guard Dog on Premises. Survivors will be Prosecuted.'

Irish Tales

Short cut
During a walking holiday in Ireland, a Newcastle woman and friend found themselves at dusk with no sign of a town in which to spend the night. They stopped a passing couple to ask where the nearest one lay and the man said: 'Well, now, 'twould be a good three miles.' Seeing the tourists' faces fall, his wife broke in: 'Ah, Michael, make it two. Can't you see they're walking?'

Double the pleasure
A Norwich reader reports that he was riding a jaunting car when a hiker asked his driver how far it was to the nearest town. 'About three miles,' he was told. As the ride continued, my correspondent protested that the distance was not less than six miles. Replied the driver: 'He'll be all the more pleased when he gets there.'

Quick march
One more Irish walking story, for the road, so to speak, about the young man who asked a passer-by how far it

was to the nearest town and was told: 'It's six miles, indeed, but to a young feller like yourself steppin' out, you'll do it in four.'

With Ireland facing a rise in its inland postal rates to 22p you can't turn round without being told that people are rushing to buy up the 18p stamps while stocks last.

Baleful plea

I don't think any British newspaper reported the court case from Cork in which two men assaulted a shopkeeper and then tried to make their escape by horse and cart. From the same court this week, the Cork *Examiner* reports:

'Mr John Geoff, Solicitor, for the defendant, handed in a medical certificate to Justice Patrick Keenan Johnson stating that he was unable to attend court. Mr Geoff said his client was suffering from a serious illness but he could not pronounce the name.'

Bless you! Goodbye!

The expenditure column in the accounts of a church in County Monaghan contains this item: 'Messrs –: £7.31, Communion wine and weedkiller.'

Loose schedule

I hear of the porter at Cork Station who was asked what time a certain train was leaving. When he answered, the questioner persisted: 'Does that mean British summer time, Greenwich mean time, or what?'

'Sure,' said the porter with an expansive wave of the arm, 'it just means God's good time.'

Tales From Overseas

Wright on!
The latest edition of the magazine *West Africa* contains this news item from Nigeria:

'The Minister of Science and Technology, Dr Sylvester Ugoh, has said that the Federal Government would give assistance to the first Nigerian to make an aircraft. Malam Mohammed Mustapha from Borno State was reported to have succeeded in assembling an aircraft from a Volkswagen engine, zinc roofing sheets, pieces of timber and plywood, light iron rods and Vespa scooter tyres.

'Dr Ugoh said that a team of experts would be sent from Lagos to Maiduguri in order to study the technological success of Malam Mustapha whom, he said, would be given all the assistance he would need to perfect his invention.'

Notice seen in the workshop of a garage near California's Yosemite Park: 'Service charge $20 an hour. $30 if you watch. $40 if you help.'

Nothing personal
Seen in a newspaper published in Hobart, Tasmania:
'A magistrate was not biased against a man he called a
clown, an idiot, a ratbag, a nit, a clot and a dickhead, the
Court of Criminal Appeal ruled. The court said the
magistrate was merely expressing an opinion he had
formed of the man.'

Mynheer, go there
Often irritated by those railway station shops which
have signs warning: 'No change for phones or ticket
machines', a colleague believes he found in Amsterdam
Central Railway Station the other day a notice
promising an all-time record in non-co-operation.

On the counter of the Dutch Railways travel bureau
was a sign in Dutch and English. 'No train information. No boat information. No international tickets.
No maps of the city. Tourist and Hotel Information –
not here.'   .

Thought for today
An article on Papua New Guinea health services in the
latest issue of *World Medicine* includes a photograph of
some natives and the caption: 'Once these people were
cannibals. Now 80 per cent of the children under five
are malnourished.'

*I hear there used to be a very popular book of good
works entitled:* A Hundred and One Ways to Serve
Humanity.

Hazy warning

Reported sign at a petrol station as one enters the Serengeti Plain in Tanzania: 'Last chance for fuel. Next three stations are mirages.'

Ve haf vays ...

Sluggish risers should be warned about the Hotel Columbus in Bremen where the room voucher carries the peremptory words: 'Breakfast ist obligatory!'

Desert Lib

Reports of casualties still being caused by abandoned wartime explosives brings word from a former serviceman in the Middle east about the change in an Arab tradition which has brought women to the fore.

Before the Second World War, a wife always walked several paces behind her husband. Since 1945 she is allowed to step out proudly in front of him.

Gark, gark

A New Zealand diplomat, recently in Rome, bought a toy dog for his granddaughter from a street vendor. Demonstrated on the pavement, it bounced and yapped.

Back in his hotel bedroom it still bounced but there was no bark. He strode back and found the salesman who apologised profusely and exchanged the toy for another one which bounced and barked.

His anger flared when, alone again, he watched the thing do its clockwork stuff in total silence. He was about to rush out and do I know not what antipodean mayhem when an Italian friend took him on one side to explain what excellent ventriloquists can be found in Rome.

It is not reported in the Guinness Book of Records, I am sorry to say, but the University of California at Berkeley is proudly reporting to visitors that it has the world's largest collection of fossilised animal dung – more than 6,000 specimens.

Red wheeler-dealer
A British woman living in Warsaw, where many goods are in short supply, tells me what happened when she found her car with a flat tyre. She took out a foot pump and was working it when two men approached. Help at last, she thought. But, no. They smiled and said: 'Can we buy the pump?'

Old Soldiers Never Lie?

Pre-history
Tales of long service were being swapped in the Chief
Petty Officers' mess at HMS Dolphin submarine base
the other day when a retired chief remarked on his stint
in the China station, which prompted a much younger
man to ask: 'How long ago?'

From the leathery-faced chief electrician came the
reply: 'He was in when Long John Silver had two legs
and an egg on his shoulder.'

Age old
A very senior serviceman has just written to say that he
was in uniform before the Dead Sea was reported sick.
Whether he is the same man who enlisted when
Nelson's Victory was still an acorn, I couldn't swear. It
used to be said that a Flight Sergeant in my RAF
squadron knew Pontius before he was a pilot. Back
home, in Bow Street police station, it is reputed there
used to be a sergeant who knew Covent Garden when it
was only a window box.

A periodic report written by an officer about a sailor in his division at a time when the midday issue of rum was a regular part of shipboard life in the Royal Navy: 'In the mornings this man is an idiot,' he wrote. 'In the afternoons he is a gibbering idiot.'

Flimsy evidence

Extracts from several 'flimsies' written about naval officers by their captains have come across my desk, such as: 'The only reason for men to follow this officer would be out of curiosity.'

There are several variations on the theme of 'carrying out his duties to his own entire satisfaction', including a remarkably resigned: 'This officer has conducted himself to my wife's entire satisfaction.'

One officer protested at a report which read: 'Has been known to return on board drunk.' His captain obligingly agreed to change it to read: 'Has been known to return on board sober.'

Final deterrent

The British Officer's Club in post-war Paris had a drink known as 'The 75' consisting of a near-lethal mixture of gin, cointreau and champagne, but its reputation still never quite matched that of a similar club which occupied the Long Bar of the Hamburg Atlantic hotel in 1945. When Montgomery was asked what punishment he would recommend for German war criminals he replied that he would take them to the Long Bar and say: 'Look what beat you!'

A verbal message from a cockney rating informed a

*Royal Navy Officer that he was to report to Ari Jaba.
The officer searched the atlas with growing alarm and
then went to collect the written directions: to Harwich
harbour.*

Drop shot

At Sandhurst the other day I heard another story about
the unique brand of wit with which Regimental
Sergeant Majors continue to terrify their charges. At a
last minute review on the parade ground before a recent
passing out parade, a cadet was unlucky enough to drop
his rifle.

RSM: 'What regiment will have the honour of
             your presence, sah?'
Cadet: 'Airborne, sir.'
RSM: 'Then your rifle should have floated down
             gently.'

Peace officers

Some British police constables, whose benign presence
helped keep relative peace during the recent elections in
Rhodesia/Zimbabwe, left their helmets behind as
souvenirs. These are now being prominently displayed
in the villages of the lucky recipients.

Long may they continue to preside over peaceful
scenes. I hope I will not break the spell by recalling the
story of the District Officer in the old days who had a
glass eye.

When he had to leave his home base temporarily he
always left the eye behind, prominently displayed on
his verandah so that the locals would know he was still
watching them!

I now hear that the District Commissioner who left his glass eye behind to watch his charges whenever he went up-country, returned one day to find all the villagers lounging about and drinking. A brave man among them had crept up behind the eye and covered it with a hat, setting them free from its unblinking surveillance.

False alarm

That District Commissioner in Africa, whose villagers discovered how to foil the glass eye he left behind to watch them, gave the problem some thought. The next time he went away he again left the eye, and a set of false teeth, too, with the warning that the first man to come too near would get bitten!

Job Lot

XI per cent already
The following advertisement recently appeared in the
Jewish Chronicle without further explanation: 'Foot-
ballers and cricketers required urgently to join our
winning team. Must be able to do PAYE, VAT,
bookkeeping and auditing.'

*NALGO, the local government union, reports that its
membership is now 750,000, with 355,757 women and
348,809 men. Presumably the other 45,434 work in the
sex discrimination industry and aren't letting on.*

Horses for courses
A young woman applicant was interviewed for a
managerial post with a Coventry company in the
presence of a man described as an industrial psy-
chologist. She got a glimpse of his notepad, which was
blank except for her name and the comment: 'Nice
teeth.'

A Situations Vacant advertisement in the British Bandsman *asks for: 'Accountant for newly established medicentre polyclinic in Riyadh, Saudi Arabia. Trombone player preferred.'*

Simple as ABC
Kent County Council staff vacancy circular No 22/79 advertises for 'Library Assistant: Dartford Division. Would suit school leaver who enjoys meeting the public. Wide variety of duties, including working with books.'

The current University of London Careers Advisory Service Guide contains an advertisement for the Kensington and Chelsea Borough Engineer's Department: 'Vacancy exists for personnel assistant . . . Would be suitable for a graduate of any discipline looking for experience in this type of work. The successful candidate should be literate.'

Who can, referees
A job application form obtained at his local council offices by a reader's seventeen-year-old son included the request: 'Give the names, addresses and professions of two referees. They should not be your schoolteachers but responsible persons of mature age who are well acquainted with you.'

A student sitting a recent City of London Polytechnic accountancy examination began to answer the first question: the preparation of a Trading, Profit and Loss and Appropriation account. His/her efforts ended abruptly on the first page with the note: 'Calculator packed up.'

Books and cooks

I am not sure who – women's lib or the auditors – ought to worry most about this advertisement in a Yorkshire newspaper: 'Part-time clerk required, able to type and with some knowledge of PAYE, VAT and general cooking.'

It is good to see the Eurocrats are meticulous with their calculators. This week's list of grants made to British regions under the EEC Regional Fund for 1979 shows for example, that northern England gets precisely £8,055,343 and 40 pence.

Djinn ex machina

It was a pleasant change to see a few smiles around the Department of Employment yesterday as they welcomed the return of the famous 'Chinese electrician'. There was a time, ten years or so ago, when this oriental djinn was reported present at every eleventh-hour management-union confrontation. Cynicism and lack of faith have driven him away, but suddenly in *The Times* report yesterday of latest moves in the steel strike, there he was again: 'CHINK OF LIGHT EMERGES ...'

Ending unemployment
Shell has an advertisement in this month's *New Civil Engineer* magazine for senior structural engineers. It declares: 'The North Sea is our business – why not drop in?'

Latest information on the British Steel Corporation cut-back on jobs to reduce its huge cash losses, comes from the Scunthorpe edition of Steel News. *This reports: 'Ralph P–, manager, information systems and stores, took early retirement at the end of March. Because of this move and because of managerial restructuring to help meet the future needs of the Scunthorpe Division, three new appointments have been announced.'*

Last edition
A reader from Walton-on-Thames, Surrey, has received this notice through his letter-box: 'As your newsagent, we are pleased to announce we can now offer you a fully comprehensive shoe repair service.'

This tribute was paid to a retiring member of the board of Cambridge United football club: 'We are sorry to lose him after his thirteen years as a director, and seven or eight years before that when he was a hard worker.'

Oh, Wilberforce!
An advertisement in the English-language newspaper

in Jeddah, Saudi Arabia, declares: 'Delivered in 30 days upon receipt of orders, 90 days warranty, return if not satisfied at our expense.' The merchandise on offer is manpower – 'name it, we have it' – from the Philippines.

Initial Letters

Take a letter

A Hampshire reader unwisely wrote back to one of
those word processors which churn out advertising
circulars making what, in earlier days, would have been
the reasonable point that it was unnecessary to
sandwich his name between a 'Mr' and an 'Esq'. The
next letter from the same monster, informing him that
he was one of 1,223 people chosen in the Emsworth area
to be included in a 'prize draw', was addressed to: 'Dear
Mr Esq...'

Some computers, I am solemnly assured, have now
been specially programmed to avoid such traps.
Perhaps this is the reason why Manchester magistrate
Fred Balcombe keeps getting letters addressed to Fred
Balco MBE.

Master of both?

The headmaster of Moyle's Court School, Hampshire,
sends me an envelope addressed to him as 'Mr G H L
Rimbault and Mr A Cantab'.

A Mr Askew from Brixham regrets having sent Reader's Digest *a business card bearing his qualifications as an Associate of the Royal Institute of Chemistry and a Member of the Institute of Biology. Ever since, he tells me, he has been inundated with blandishments calculated to result in goods being delivered to, or prize cars being parked outside, 'your home at ARICMI Biol.'*

DIY at FCO
Steve Hiscock, second secretary at our embassy in Islamabad, subscribed to *Reader's Digest* and has his copy sent to the Foreign and Commonwealth Office (FCO) mailing service in London to be forwarded to him. He has just been invited to compete for a prize which would enable him to 'Buy a new car ... Move to a new house, or redecorate and refurnish FCO, King Charles Street from top to bottom ...'

Just so
When R W Brady of Fowey got on to the Automobile Association computer it added an initial, making him R G W Brady. He altered this in ink on one of its forms: 'not G just R W'. His membership card duly arrived, made out to Mr G Just R.W.

The latest example I have from the world of word processing machines is the unisex Mrs ... Esq, but curious forms of address have been with us for many years. I hear that when Prince Philip served in HMS Wallace in 1942 he was officially listed as Lt. Philip P.o.G (for Prince of Greece). All his laundry used to come back marked Lt. Pog.

Noble address

An envelope returned by a 'temp' typist to a City executive was addressed to:

    Sir Horace Cutler The Greater
    London Council
    County Hall
    London SE1

Even greater

Sir Horace Cutler, Leader of the Greater London Council, has now attracted one of those mindless letters from a computer addressed to: 'Sr Horace C. Obe.' I am not sure whether Sir Horace is more worried about having his designation made a surname or his title transformed into that of a Spanish grandee.

Real nobility

The typist who wrote to Sir Horace Cutler the Greater at London Council must take second place in the grandeur of her imagination to the author of an envelope to the Registrar of Births, Deaths and Marriages in Newport, Shropshire. This was addressed to: The Registrar of Life and Death.

They still have a pretty line in social distinctions in East Anglia. The editor of the East Anglian Magazine *tells me he has received two identical letters from a firm of Wisbech seedsmen. One, addressed to him as gardening correspondent, starts 'Dear Mr J. G. L. Spence'. The other, to him as editor, begins: 'Dear J. G. L. Spence Esq'.*

73

Red letter days

As word spread at a recent diplomatic party in Rome that Mark Heath, the British Minister at the Holy See, had been made a Knight Commander of the Royal Victorian order, a lady was heard to ask: 'Is it true that Mr Heath is now a Sir?' Yes, she was told.

'Does that mean,' she persisted, 'that when I write to him I have to put K G B after his name?'

Luckless

Buzzed
Seen in a lay-by in Derbyshire, a French car with a sticker in the back window stating: 'I'm buzzing along for free enterprise.' The occupant was beside the car, changing the wheel.

Ow!
A Hampshire reader who was not too happy with his car registration letters COW, recently traded it in. His new car is SOW.

Waiting arms
Thanks to a newspaper in Maidenhead I learn of the squatter who discovered an empty house in excellent condition on Court House Road. Barely had he settled in, however, when the tramp of heavy feet was heard. It turned out to be a police house awaiting a newly promoted occupant.

A commuting friend who had his car stolen twice from

Peterborough Station car park finally bought an old banger for his station trips and fitted a safety lock, too. A week later thieves stole the lock.

I now hear from another friend, even more deeply shamed, when he found that his brand-new car had been broken into and nothing taken but some musical cassettes.

From a reader, even deeper shame: returning to his one-year-old car after a seminar in Birmingham he discovered it had been broken into. The only thing removed was the car park ticket.

Thoughtful to the end

From New York I hear of an obituary notice in a local newspaper which ended with: 'Members of the family kindly request mourners to omit floral tributes. The deceased was allergic to flowers.'

Salad days

Roger Banfield, executive chef at the Cafe Royal, described one of his greatest culinary disasters during a reception in which his restaurant was given an award by Wedgwood for its gastronomic excellence. 'At an important dinner I mixed up the cream and the mayonnaise,' he said shamelessly, 'and all the guests were served strawberries covered in mayonnaise.'

Even slower

I am indebted to the Rev George McCutcheon of the Manse, Clackmannan, for the report of a letter delivered to Balquhidder Manse recently. It was a circular advertising at £20 a copy a well-known business directory with the slogan 'Out of date information is costly'. The addressee was: R. McGregor, Balguidder (sic), Perthshire. Rob Roy died in 1734.

Not enough
Overheard from a woman at the Nature Conservancy at Hastingleigh: 'The notice says Wildlife Nature Reserve and all I can see are sheep.'

Cold comfort
A Florida man was rushed to hospital after a snake bit him on the finger. Doctors removed the poison, saved the finger, and told him to stick it in an ice pack. Two weeks later the finger had to be amputated because of frostbite.

A Middlesex reader tells me that her son spent the first precious fifteen minutes of his mock O Level in Maths looking for somewhere to sit. Asked why there weren't enough desks for all the examination candidates, the Headmaster said: 'The Head of Maths miscalculated.'

Small massacre ...
Not many hurt, the heading in the South Wales *Echo* should have said in reporting that 'Zulu', a re-enactment of the Zulu wars, had its opening night at the Sherman Arena Theatre, Cardiff, cancelled because of an accident. 'Patrick Barlow fell off a chair ... while he and his co-star, Julian Hough, were impersonating an army of 100,000.'

Pardon?

Are ewe hungry?
From the Church News section of the *West Sussex Gazette*: 'The churchyard of West Funtington has been divided into five acres in an attempt to enlist volunteers to help with its maintenance. One acre will be grazed by the vicar's sheep: it is hoped to have at least three or four human volunteers for each of the other areas.'

If wet...
'The air defences of Great Britain will be realistically tested', declares a Ministry of Defence announcement, 'when aircraft of the Royal Air Force and the air forces of six other nations take part in Exercise Priory on 15 and 16 October with 17 October as a reserve day in case of bad weather.'

A smart young man was seen going into Marconi-Elliot's space electronics research centre in south Hertfordshire the other day carrying a boomerang.

Controlled flight

From a Surrey parish magazine: 'The winner of the competition to guess the number of sweets in the jar was Miss – who will, therefore, travel to Majorca by air, spend two nights in a luxury hotel (all inclusive) and fly home via Paris without needing to spend a penny.'

Forever Irish

Tony O' Reilly, darling of British rugby in the 1950s, now president of H J Heinz in Pittsburg, has not lost his sense of humour during his ten years in America. He delighted an audience of businessmen by relating how he and various other British Lions staggered out of a New Zealand bar late one night. The great Welshman Ray Prosser turned to him and said: 'Tony, you drive. You're far too drunk to sing.'

Verb. sap.

When Margaret Winfield, the Liberal Party president, was asked if she thought there would be much interest in the party's leadership contest, she replied: 'There are more people interested in this than there are in politics.'

Chauvinist sequitur

From *Labour Weekly* on James Callaghan's origins: 'Either way he does not have much Irish blood in him. His father died when he was 9 and it was his mother who brought him up.'

It can't be true – or can it? – that when the question 'Who or What is Devolution?' was put to the people of a small community in South Wales, 10 per cent said he was Jeremiah's brother, 10 per cent that it was an aria from 'Elijah', 10 per cent that it was the last book of the Bible, and the remainder that he was a French prop forward.

Cash difference
There seems to be shocking discrimination going on at Ramsey Golf Club in the Isle of Man. An advertisement for staff states: 'The Steward will be responsible for running the bar. The Stewardess will be responsible for catering and taking the profits.'

Returned unopposed
A farmer was asked in a Norfolk pub about a skull his son had unearthed while ditch digging. After a long pull on his pint, he replied slowly: 'It was the thickest skull I've ever seen. We sent it to the council.'

Spreading the word
A major demonstration of what to do with farm waste is opening at the National Agricultural Centre, Stoneleigh. The organisers promise: 'Muck '80 will be more comprehensive than ever – covering virtually the whole range of equipment and machinery currently available.'

Just so
At a recent meeting in London of a United Nations committee on chemical matters, the American delegation was asked why its senior member was not

present. 'Today we've got distributable intelligence instead of hierarchical control,' came the explanation.

Got a big family?
An advertisement for Funeral Operatives in a Colchester newspaper offers: 'Good rates of pay and staff discount.'

On Offer

A drop in the ocean
A colleague has just received an announcement from a
Hampshire firm of boat builders. Casually attached to
the bottom of the page is a tear-off slip saying: 'Please
send me ... yachts at the 1980 Autumn price of £28,000 +
VAT.'

Safety in numbers?
A New York reader tells me that he is surprised to see
that the Pill, which his wife has been buying in boxes of
25, is now available in boxes of 50 marked 'Twin Pack'.

Going, going ...
Sign outside a Wiltshire do-it-yourself shop: 'Special
Offer. Disappearing loft ladders. Only two left.'

*One of those joke shops has been successfully selling
'genuine Irish mugs' recently. They are just like
everybody else's except that the handle is on the inside.
An attempt to replenish the stock, however, produced*

*the reply: 'We are very sorry but the Japanese firm that
supplied them has discontinued the line.'*

Exactly
Advertisers, shifting their sights from TV to newspaper
audiences, clearly feel they can take no chances on the
literacy of prospective buyers. I have just been sent a
large, printed invitation to buy curtains, with the
warning: ORDER TWO if pair required.

Take your pick
Notice on a Herts farm gate: 'Horse manure 30p a bag or
à la carte.'

Tight lisped
A New Year sale sign over a pile of tights on a
Birmingham market stall: 'Will fit all thighzes.'

*'Lovely turkey for sale' says an advert in a Sussex paper.
Not a particularly unusual offer, perhaps – except that
it appeared in the Pets column.*

Watch dog
Seen in a newsagent's shop near Holland Park: 'Dog for
sale, Eats anything. Fond of children.'

A reader recently put a literary advertisement in The
Times *offering: 'For sale, 76 King Penguins.' He had
two replies, both from livestock dealers.*

Refinement

From the catalogue of a New York bookseller: 'This is one of the rarest works on cannibalism (with 10 plates cloth).'

Brr'm brr'm

This advertisement appeared in a long-established nudists' magazine: 'Naturist's Motor Cycle for sale. Fur saddle and vacuum flask holder. Solar heated crash helmet. Will exchange for clothes.'

On The Dark Side

Cignal warning
Sign in a bedroom of a small Sussex hotel: 'Please do not smoke in bed or the next lot of ashes to fall on the floor may be yours.'

His and...
The woodwork master at a Wiltshire school tells me that, when he asked the boys in his junior class to make a model vehicle of some kind during the Christmas holidays, sixteen returned with model cars and ten with model lorries. One made a model hearse.

In the offices attached to a south London crematorium there is a large notice listing: Important Telephone Numbers. The first one is: Serious Burns Unit.

Light reading
A Brighton crematorium has a waiting-room for mourners who arrive early. There is a pile of magazines for them to read – all copies of *Sussex Life*.

Cut to the quick

Letter in a Norfolk school magazine: 'Dear Editor, I was very distressed to read in your Spring issue a note recording the death of Walter Brown. Of all the Old Boys I knew, he was undoubtedly the one I most admired. I cannot believe that he is no longer with us. Yours sincerely, Walter Brown.'

Down to earth

Sign in a Camberwell pub: 'Please do not throw your cigarette ends on the floor as they may burn those ladies and gentlemen who leave here on hands and knees.'

Speaking to a building workers' conference in a debate on death benefits an Irish delegate declared: 'They say you can't take it with you when you go and it is a matter of regret that this benefit is only paid to a member when he has died.'

Ever after

Sign seen in my local pub: 'Don't drink if you're driving. There is no cure for the mourning after.'

Old precedent

Alec Bedser's tart comment at the Man of the Year lunch given by the Royal Association for Disability and Rehabilitation, on the apparent practice of honouring only batsmen like Hobbs, Hutton and Bradman with cricketing knighthoods: 'The last bloody bowler to be knighted was Sir Francis Drake.'

Fair Cops

Down the plug hole
Thieves yesterday stole a van containing £7,000 worth of soap and toiletries in Rochdale. The police report said: 'They got clean away.'

Look before you...
Wives, it must be admitted, do not drive at their best with a husband in the passenger seat. So it was, in Bristol a little while ago, that when a wife drove her husband home from an anniversary dinner her nervousness attracted the attention of a roving police patrol.

On being waved down, the husband stepped from the car and was promptly given a breathalyser test. Examining the tell-tale crystals, the officer then spoke the necessary ritual, advising him that he was over the limit and therefore liable to prosecution.

Police officers in Bristol may by now, I think, have been warned to check first whether the cars they stop are left-hand drive or not.

The Chief Constable of Bedfordshire tells me that he was pleased but not altogether sure he should be flattered by a letter of thanks from a local women's organisation. This referred not only to the tactful behaviour of his officers but also to the prompt arrival of their 'pander car'.

Too true!
From the *Bexhill News*: 'Thieves broke into a Bexhill undertakers in the dead of night last week...'

No objection
Judge Alan King-Hamilton yesterday finished a lengthy trial at Luton during which he frequently travelled to and fro on the same train as some of the barristers in the case.

One day towards the end of the trial he took aside one of the junior counsel and said: 'When I got on at Radlett this morning I looked all round and couldn't see any of you.'

'Perhaps, your honour,' said the young barrister, 'that was because our train didn't stop at Radlett.'

'Yes,' the judge conceded after a moment's thought. 'And that, if I may say so, is the best point you've made in the entire trial.'

Police in Manchester clearly believe in giving prisoners a fair chance. In Trafford borough council's planning applications, the Chief Constable applies to equip his Stretford Division HQ with an escape staircase.

Frozen asset
From the *Kent & Sussex Courier*: 'Mrs Christine O–, of
Golden Green, who was tied to a refrigerator door at
gunpoint by two raiders, has been praised for her
coolness by Tonbridge police.'

Caught hymn
'Choirboy caught betting' proclaimed a poster outside a
West Midlands newsagent's shop. To which someone
had added: 'Ah, those sweet childish trebles.'

*Motoring southwards from Chipping Ongar, Essex,
the other day, a reader saw one of those big boards at the
roadside warning: 'POLICE – ACCIDENT.' Twenty
yards further on there was a police car in the ditch.*

Grassed
A recent seizure of a consignment of cannabis by police
and customs officers was proudly described as a 'joint
operation'.

Over-policed
Drivers in Suffolk, it is reported, are eight times more
likely to be prosecuted for using defective vehicles than
those on Merseyside. Could this, I am asked, be because
it is Constable country?

Heaven protect us
Greater Manchester police 'Bulletin' reports a traffic
accident which involved a car containing four nuns. PS

Steve Arden recounts that it was the first time he had seen an innocent driver go up to the offending driver and say: 'Oh, dearie me, what happened?'

Perhaps the police are feeling the pressure of a new tourist season. An extract from the City of London police complaints' register, as reported in the force's monthly magazine, reads: 'City gent (somewhat infirm): Officer, can you see me across the road? Constable: Nip across and I'll tell you.'

Hold on

I see from the Leicester *Mercury* that a youth who was found hanging by his fingertips from the window of a rubbish chute room more than 150 ft up was persuaded to clamber to safety by policewoman Sheila Onions. Not surprisingly, some earlier efforts by two of her male colleagues had failed. 'They offered him cigarettes and coffee but he kept on refusing.'

Could You Re-Phrase That?

Advice for tourists
In the National Westminster Bank Pocket Guide to London it says: 'If you are lost in London, telephone 222 1234 (London Transport), tell them where you are and they will tell you where to go.'

Seeing they're fed
The Electrical Contractors' Association invitation to a conference in Surrey on Wednesday adds that discussion will be followed by a light lunch.

Several readers have seen fit to draw my attention to Richmond's 'Irish recipe: thick sausages'.

Winking at danger
Notice seen over a lathe in the woodwork classroom of a Gloucestershire comprehensive school: 'Protect your eyes. One pupil only at this machine.'

Dab on Dobbin
Certain perfumes of Laura Ashley were advertised in a Sunday newspaper as 'certain to evoke the tradition of the English countryside, providing a stable fragrance which lasts throughout the day'.

Daniel Topolski, coach for the Olympic women's eight rowing team, is quoted as saying that he chose the Exeter canal at Countess Wear for training because it is 'beautifully flat.'

Alliterate
The Bishop's message in the latest issue of the Peterborough Diocese News begins: 'There is singularly little missionary strategy planned and postulated upon preconceived opinions posing as principles in the Acts of the Apostles...'

Fun for all
This notice was posted in a Berkshire village hall: 'Coming Events. Tuesday, July 22. No W.I. whist drive.'

Barefaced challenge
A notice seen in Tiverton, Devon: 'Tennis shoes *only* must be worn on courts.' It is suggested that, in view of Brighton Council's decision to set aside a beach for nudists, Devon is trying to become more actively daring.

A passenger studying the lunch menu on an Air India

flight bringing some English tourists back from Delhi to London was heard to say: 'I really ought to have the curry, but I just don't have the guts.'

Wash-day blues?
A sign outside a West Midlands pub proclaimed: 'Good Clean Entertainment Every Night Except Monday.'

Scooping the pool
From Stone, the Stafford *News Letter* reports that women swimmers have complained about the lack of curtains on the changing cubicles. 'John Ferris, vice-chairman of the Alleyne's Sport Centre Management Committee, told the council meeting: "Leave it with me. I will look into it".'

English usage
A notice listing mealtimes at the door of an English languages school for foreigners in Oxford concludes with the request: 'After your meal, please return your used food.'

A reader tells me he has just had a letter from an Israeli teacher who recently visited him in London, asking for 'the name of the Church of England we passed that was right beside the Hammersmith Passover'.

Short and sweet
From a letter to parents from a Somerset school: 'The Parents' Association has arranged for a representative

of the Association on Alcoholism to speak at the school. He is an excellent speaker and will probably be willing to have a "quick one" with some of us after the evening is over.'

A Bournemouth reader, recently 65, has been allocated a rather tactless pension number by the Department of Health. It is 0585197 DIE.

Name Dropping

Asses to Worms

Every now and then a reader spots a curious conjunction of names and occupation and passes it on to me. It was rather overwhelming, however, to receive a collection of 4,000 unusual names all in one parcel.

Doris Rutherford, 71, of Worthing, spent six years collecting them and listing them under categories. For example:

Animals: Ass, A'bear, Badger, Beaver (and Beevers), Boa, Buck, Bunney, Bull, Bullock, Cairns, Callf, Camel, Capon, Catt, Cattle, Chick, Chicken, Collie (and Colley), Coney, Cow, Curr, Deer, Dragon, Dobbin, Doe, Dolphin, Eland, Fawn, Ferret, Fido, Foale, Fox, Game, Gibbon, Goosey, Hack, Hare, Hart, Heffer, Hind, Hogg, Horsey, Hunter, Kitcat, Lamb (and Lambkin), Leveritt, Lion (and Lyons), Mares, Mole, Mules, Mutton, Otter, Pointer, Rabbit, Ram, Roebuck, Sables, Seal, Squirrel, Stag, Stallion, Steer, Stoate, Suckling, Tiger, Turtle, Whale, Wildbore, Wolf and Worms.

That is just one of the 52 headings Mrs Rutherford has used. There are 54 afflictions, 34 virtues, 45 vices, 80 each of household wares and eatables, 76 articles of clothing and 46 exclamations like Bravo, Heck, Odam, Cursham, Basham, Sorrie and Pardon.

During the last financial year I see that legacies were left to the Royal Society for the Protection of Birds by Mrs Bird, Mr Nightingale, Miss Partridge, Mrs Swift, Mrs Wildgoose – and Mr Fox.

Promotion
Mr Clarke was recently appointed Manager of National Westminster Bank's branch at the Isle of Dogs. Before that he was Assistant Manager, Barking.

Prolific
Heard from a middle-aged woman in the kitchen department of an Oxford Street store: 'I tell you one thing. This Pat Pending fellow sure comes up with a lot of new gadgets.'

The Pending family
Boris Harris, former concerts director of the London Philharmonic Orchestra recalls for me that talented musician, Conductor Pending.

The phrase is used when advertising concerts before confirmation of the conductor's availability has been received. 'But a great myth grew up about the Scandinavian conductor, Pending,' says Harris. 'I even heard a youngster discussing his reading of Sibelius's second symphony.'

A former secretary of the Old Dunstonians Rugby Club tells me that before the Second World War he was regularly in a position to select a back row of Wild, Savage and Rough.

In German?
An advertisement for the recent Seaford Festival of the Arts declared that Seaford Choral Society was to perform 'Handelssohn's "Elijah".'

Plain ailing
A cruiser recently registered at a Cheshire sailing club has been named 'Cirrhosis of the River'.

How wrong can you get? Among the names listed at Marlborough Street court in London were Barry Bright for stealing and Trevor Genius for attempting to steal.

Real names
A final 1979 selection of names includes the following:
  Chosen to represent the bricklayers at the re-opening of Priory Church, Doncaster – Mr B. Heavenly.
  The Director of Statistics at the Department of Education and Science – K. G. Forecast.
  Plymouth Adult Education Centre's 'class for those who are interested in singing in friendly company'. Apply Mrs N. S. Screech.
  An article on 'Laxatives: widely used and abused' in *Pulse*, the medical journal, is by Dr A Li Wan Po.
  Not to mention that some time ago in Hornchurch, a Miss Tough married her Mr Savage!

Since my report of a greengrocer's shop named Melon-Cauli, I have heard that there is a garage in Northumberland called Tyred and Exhausted.

Classic encounter

When Meonstoke met Trinity in a local Hampshire cricket league match the home side were out for 45 (Shakespeare 8 for 20). Trinity were skittled for only 35 (Marlow 9 for 14).

A local newspaper has just announced: ' "Ghosts", by Henry Gibson will be Burnt Ash Drama Association's entry for the Bromley Festival . . .' I wonder if anyone is entering 'The Threepenny Opera' by that well-known Lancastrian, Bert Oldbreck?

Just good friends

I see from the Ruislip and Northwood *Gazette* that a speaker from the National Dairy Council enlivened a recent meeting of the Ruislip Afternoon Towns-women's Guild with his talk on 'My Best Friend'.

He took his listeners back to 'the good old days of farming, when cows were milked by hand and he knew every one of them by name'. The aim, he said, 'was to keep his best friends, the cows, happy and contented'.

Inevitably, perhaps the speaker's name was Mr Bull.

Philosophical Asides

Fancied entry
Overheard in a Brighton bar: 'Did you sell any of your paintings at that art club show?' – 'No, but I felt quite encouraged. Somebody stole one.'

The optimist
A welfare secretary for a north London organisation received a letter asking if it was possible to carry a card saying: 'In case of accident the hospital can use my heart to help someone less fortunate.'

Holey
Sign in the rear window of an old car abandoned in a field near Basingstoke: 'Born 1962. Died 1978. Rust in peace.'

The Rev Rodham Dowson of Selsey Methodist Church in Sussex tells of the day last month when the north wind blew and the rain poured down on the launching ceremony of Selsey's new lifeboat. 'An undertaker, a policeman and a parson were standing together,' he begins in classic style.

'One of the first two looked up to the heavens and said
to the parson: "He isn't answering your prayers today."
Replied the parson: "If he always answered my prayers
you two would be redundant".'

Sad truth
Reported from Berkshire, one of those roadside notices
declaring: 'Laugh and the World Laughs with You.'
Alongside has been pencilled: 'Cry and you get what
you want.'

Memorial bust
Overheard on a Reading bus, a man of perhaps 75
saying to a friend: 'When I die I hope to be in debt,
'cause if you don't owe anybody anything they'll never
remember you, but if you owe 'em fifty quid they'll
remember you forever.'

Last word
Graffito in Green Park underground station: 'Nuclear
War – Who Cares?' Underneath another hand has
scrawled: 'Once you've seen one you've seen them all.'

Good Health!

Warning note
St John Ambulance's course for industrial first aid in
north London includes in its programme an intensive
session entitled: 'Practical (fractures)', interrupted by
just fifteen minutes for 'Break'.

...and for appendix?
I am indebted to *World Medicine* magazine for this
Middlesex Hospital catering department memo:
'Patients wishing to order Pancakes should tick the box
marked Apple Flan & Custard and likewise patients
ordering Jelly & Ice Cream should mark the Fruit Salad
box.'

*A cost conscious hospital invited staff to submit ideas
for economies and offered a £1,000 prize for the best
suggestion. One of the first notes received said: 'Cut the
prize to £250.'*

Fast learner

An apprentice at a Gloucestershire firm had a minor accident on his motor cycle and was given a certificate by his doctor for immediate sick leave. Undeterred by such formalities, he came into work and asked his supervisor if the leave could start the following Monday. 'Why so?' inquired the boss. 'Oh,' came the reply, 'there's a booze-up I want to go to on Friday.'

Grounds for decision

An article on 'Humanism in Medicine' by an American contributor to the *Lancet* includes this passage:

'One way of catching class attention is to ask what advice students would give when presented with the following family history. The father has syphilis, the mother tuberculosis, they already have had four children – the first is blind, the second died, the third is deaf and dumb and the fourth has tuberculosis.

'The mother is pregnant with her fifth child and the parents are willing to have an abortion should you so decide. Assuming there aren't too many Catholics in the class, you will usually find a majority in favour of abortion.

'You congratulate the class on their decision . . . and then tell them they have just murdered Beethoven.'

Church pillars (RV)

From the current issue of a Devon parish magazine: 'The world now has so many problems that if Moses came down from Mount Sinai today the two tablets he carried would be aspirins.'

The doctor's magazine, **Pulse,** *reports that a* GP *in Sutton Coldfield has been bequeathed a dozen boxes of fine, expensive Havana cigars. The same ex-patient also left £3,000 for cancer research.*

Hey, nanny – no!
It is reported in the St Helier *Hospital News* that a patient recently asked a ward sister if his 'old nanny' could come and visit him. She was not amused when the ward doors opened and in was led an elderly nanny-goat on the end of a rope.

Beta that!
Opticians are used to customers who come to them with broken dentures or requests for twin monocles. Into a London waiting-room the other day came an elderly Greek woman with her grandson, who explained that, as she could speak no English, he would translate for her. He was very conscientious and began with the letters on the sight test card.

Chestnut filling?
I've heard of the Chinese dentist who always made his appointments for 2.30, but this is new to me: a sign in the entry to a New York building: 'Dental Surgeon. 2th Floor.'

A new hospital opening in Kings Lynn next month has its wards named after local villages. None can be more apt than Feltwell, some twenty miles away.

Miaowt of reach
Recent discussions on television about breast-versus-bottle feeding reminds a Bexleyheath reader of the schoolgirl who wrote, after a lesson on a similar topic: 'Breast feeding is best because it contains all the nutriments needed for the baby, is the right temperature, and is the most hygienic because the cat can't get at it.'

Crazy like a fox
There is worry here at times about where some of our National Insurance funds go but I have yet to see the sort of claim recently reported from Sydney, Australia. This concerned a psychiatrist who had charged the equivalent of £1,000 a month for treating two of his colleagues.

Further inquiries produced a statement from the Voluntary Health Insurance Association, representing private medical funds, which said it had just discovered one psychiatrist who had 423 consultations with another over a two-year period.

If at first . . .
First prize in a competition run by a magazine called *Successful Slimming* is a 'luxury Caribbean cruise for two'. Second prize is a rowing machine.

A poster seen in Oswestry advertised a talk: 'Successful Family Planning.' To this someone had added: 'All you need is NO how.'

Child's proof
A harassed grandmother was struggling to open one of
those bottles of pills with a modern safety cap. Her
small granddaughter came to the rescue with: 'Let me
do it, Gran. They're the new sort to keep children from
getting at them.'

Pointed advice
The label on a bottle of pills with a safety screw-top
carries this sinister instruction: 'Line up the arrows and
push off.'

Beware of the...
This sign was seen in the outer office of a Hampshire
veterinary surgeon: 'Please do not put your pets on the
receptionist's desk – she bites.'

False Colours

Devilish clever
The leprachaun, a leading character in Irish myth-
ology, has turned out – in one case at least – to be yet
another Anglo-Saxon invader of the Emerald Isle. A
reader tells me that when his five-year-old son bought
one of the little fellows in a Galway shop he removed
the price tag to find the following inscription in Gaelic
underneath: 'An Bhreaten Mor a dheanta.' The
translation is: 'Made in Great Britain.'

Flying the flag
On a visit to Florida, a correspondent decided to buy a
scale model of the NASA space shuttle, Enterprise.
Taking it home he discovered it was made in Hong
Kong.

National pride
In a spell of patriotism, a Briton visiting the Concorde
lounge at Kennedy airport, New York, gave close
inspection to the models of the supersonic airliner
being sold there. Under the tailplane in blue letters he
found the words: 'Made in Japan.'

Situation saved

Evan Dobelle, American chief of protocol at the White House, says he had one of the best lessons in his delicate art in the shape of the story of a dinner for Commonwealth heads of state, given some years ago.

His British equivalent saw a guest pocket a gold salt shaker, told Winston Churchill what had happened and asked what to do.

'Leave it to me,' said Churchill, and proceeded to pocket a gold pepper shaker. He then turned to the guilty party and whispered: 'Oh dear, the chief of protocol saw us. We'd better put them both back.' Both embarrassment and financial loss were duly averted.

Court and Unsocial

Fact of life
A letter from a north London reader: 'My daughter came home from school recently and told me that a girl in her class was going to have a baby. I was shocked, then said: "Won't the boy marry her?" To this she answered: "Oh, he wants to marry her, but she won't marry him. She doesn't like him." '

Times are getting (relatively) harder I know, but it was still surprising to read a report in the Loughborough Echo *which concluded: 'After their reception ... the couple returned to a honeymoon at home in the garden.'*

Manly thoughts
Reported seen on a wall of a Hampshire club: 'Are you a man or a mouse?' Underneath someone had written: 'My wife is afraid of mice.'

108

Not working wife
An American businessman who is here recruiting staff for a London office tells me that a middle-aged Englishwoman's job application described her marital status as 'So-so'.

Comprehensive cover
One of the items on a price list of 'Clothes for Your Honeymoon' from a West Midlands store is: Silk and lace nightdress (in case).

In the column headed News of Old Girls in a Wiltshire school magazine I am told a wedding was reported with the note that the honeymoon was spent 'walking in the Lake District. It rained every day but they loved every minute of it and were soon resigned to looking completely bedraggled.'

First things first
The present Duke of Beaufort, who continues the family's devotion to the hunt, recalls the story that in April, 1900, his father greeted the meet at Burton, Gloucestershire, with the words: 'Before we go off to draw, I thought you would like to know that early this morning my wife gave birth to a son.'

When his huntsman suggested three cheers, the Duke's reply was abrupt: 'Certainly not! You might frighten the hounds!'

Presence of mind
A teacher at a special school in Buckinghamshire asked

which of the senior boys would like to be present at the birth of any children they might have after they were married. One would not commit himself. Pressed for his opinion, he finally said: 'Well, Miss, it depends if I know the girl very well.'

Love and marriage
An advertisement in the Kent and Sussex *Courier*: Young couple require unfurnished accommodation, marrying June, no children...

Advertisement in a Wirral newspaper: 'Unattached feminine female, attractive, intelligent and articulated, seeks male and female friendship 40+ (with transport) ...' But, of course!

LUV 4X
Advertisement in the Lancashire *Evening Telegraph*, coinciding with the issue of the new 'X' vehicle registration letter: '32-year-old male wishes to meet lady with car in return for love and affection, would appreciate photo of car...'

Till death...
From a California newspaper: 'She saw one man lying on the floor with blood streaming from his head and four men were fighting with broken bottles. About twenty women were hitting each other. "It was the worst fight I have ever seen at a wedding," she said.'

Chivalrous husband

A reader reports that in a Cowes restaurant the other day a waiter tripped and spilled hot sauce on his daughter's back. 'Her resourceful husband immediately threw a jug of iced water over her. Another girl at our table remarked: "And they say the age of chivalry is dead!" '

Degrees of blue

According to the Cambridge *Evening News* a local carpet salesman has been advising a colleague not to spend too much on expensive flooring. His reasoning is simple: 'After five years of living in Cambridge people either move or get divorced.'

As Reported

Father William Thames
An advertisement feature in a Reading newspaper, which seems to have been placed by Henley Town Council, puts a fascinating new slant on geography.

'Henley', it states, 'is sited on a corner of the Thames and there's no doubt the river dominates the town. By the time it reaches Henley it has left the roar and bustle of the Port of London far behind and is rolling north into the Chilterns.'

Finally to debouch majestically into its source, I suppose!

Sent to the Head?
From the Brighton *Evening Argus*: 'But the problem of preventing schoolroom violence is a far larger one. Capital punishment is allowed in most schools but teachers are reluctant to use it.'

Mournful headline above a council report in the Avon County Gazette: 'Gravedigging a dying craft.'

Animal crackers?
It is pure coincidence that I received in my post
yesterday a *Kentish Gazette* headline: 'Top fat stock
show prize for schoolgirl,' and another from the
Western Gazette: 'Girl takes top rabbit show prize.' At
least, I hope it is coincidence and that those girls
haven't been up to something in the chemistry lab.

*In the lost and found column of a South African
newspaper: 'One white Rabbi, with brown ears. Found
hopping down 3rd Avenue...'*

Body of protest
One of those news reports that make you pause and read
again appeared in the Suffolk *Free Press* a few days ago.
It began: 'An undertaker whose plans for a funeral
parlour in a shopping precinct have met with stiff
opposition...'

The Hong Kong news magazine Asiaweek, *in its
account of the Dacca airliner hi-jacking: 'Thus began a
134-hour odyssey of terror which was to last six days...'*

Standing quiz
From the latest *Radio Times:* 11.30 Wildlife. Can you
tell us why birds such as flamingos, ducks and waders so
often rest on only one leg? Our carefully balanced team
of naturalists answers your questions.

A reporter on a distinguished West Country newspaper

wrote a most thrilling story of the rescue of a French schoolgirl, trapped to her waist in mud as the tide rose higher and higher. She was saved, he declared, because she was able to shout the only two words of English that she knew: 'May-day... May-day...'

Keeping cool

From the Milton Keynes *Express*: 'In a report of a court case last week in which a footballer was fined for assaulting a referee we quoted Mrs –, chairman of the magistrates, as saying: "How the hell do you think we are going to get order on the terraces with your sort of behaviour." The first words should have read: "How on earth do you think..."'

Under Angmering district news in the West Sussex Gazette *appeared this paragraph: 'In last week's WSG we reported the formation of a fund-raising group called SCOTCH based at the Spotted Cow in Angmering. We would like to point out that SCOTCH stands for Spotted Cow Organisation to Create Help, and not Hell, as we stated.'*

Tricky

This announcement in a north Yorkshire company's house journal would seem to add a whole new dimension to the art of puzzle solving: 'CROSSWORD. Space constraints made it impossible to include a crossword in this issue. However, the results will appear in next month's edition, with the prize-winners.'

Well done
From the Bath *Evening Chronicle:* 'Milkman Tony Jacob was the toast of Hinton Charterhouse today after rescuing a man of 68 from a blazing cottage...'

Nursing Officer Ray Lightning of Dereham was struck in the eye by a twig but still played the piano for eight hours in a charity marathon, reports an East Anglian daily newspaper. The only missed opportunity seems to have been by the sub-editor who failed to headline the story: Lightning Struck by Tree.

Shop Talk

Dead unlucky
'Do you have any condolence cards?' a Birmingham reader asked a woman assistant in her local newsagent's shop. 'No, dear,' came the reply, 'we don't stock any games at all.'

A dog's chance
Notice at the entrance to Woolworth's in Eastbourne: 'No smoking, guide dogs excepted.'

Good question
A Salisbury reader went into a local bookshop recently and asked the assistant if she had a copy of Sir Kenneth Clark's *Civilisation*. She replied: 'I don't know. What's it about?'

Christmas shopping in Colchester, a correspondent asked for a set of crib figures. The assistant looked puzzled, then replied: 'Oh, no, we only have sets of chess and backgammon.'

Off Pat
A Sussex holidaymaker, back from the Greek Islands, asked at her local library for a book about Patmos. 'Sorry,' she was told, 'but we do have something on Stirling Moss.'

Revised version
'Have you a book of conversion tables?' a Sussex bookshop assistant was asked. 'I'm afraid not,' came the reply. 'The only thing we stock in that line is the Bible.'

I wonder why?
A Cornish reader who looked for a diamond wedding card in an Exeter greeting card shop, found only two, and asked if there were any more. 'I'm sorry, madam,' said the assistant, 'but they are not very popular.'

Ivor Spencer, President of the Guild of Professional Toastmasters, tells me he has just had a telephone call from what sounded like an irate Asian demanding a replacement for a faulty toaster he bought in Oxford Street.

Stranger on the shore
A Middle East visitor went into a travel and theatre ticket booking agency in Worthing and asked for two tickets for Acker Bilk, whose band was shortly to appear locally. Did he want single or return tickets, asked the assistant, and exactly where was this place?

For a birdie?

A department store advertisement in Beverley, east Yorkshire, announces 'Something Special' in its new sports shop: 'Men's Golf Shirts from £7.99. Matching skirts £9.95.'

A Camberley clergyman, properly dressed, was somewhat taken aback when a cheery shop assistant asked, as she wrapped his purchase: 'And are you going away for Christmas, sir?'

No Answer To That

Justice
Barrister at Bradford Crown Court: If prison it now must be, it could be adequately dealt with by a sentence reckoned in months rather than years.

Judge: The sentence will be 30 months.

Self-service
Written on a poster in a Sussex social security office: 'If you need a helping hand, there's one at the end of your arm.'

Kindly light
P.C. John Williams stopped a clergyman driving on an East Lancashire road one evening because a front sidelight was not working. When the officer pointed this out, the clergyman replied: 'Oh, my God!' The light immediately came on again.

When asked if it was the council's intention to close the Empire Theatre, Sunderland, the leisure committee

chairman replied, according to the Newcastle Evening
Chronicle: *'The answer is an affirmative no.'*

Scenic route

A young taxi driver was heard boasting to the barmaid
in a Fulham pub: 'I had a smashing trip today. Picked
up a couple of Americans in Holborn at eleven, took
them to Oxford and back and dropped them at the
Savoy.'

Barmaid: 'Really, dear? Did they ask to go that way
round?'

No foundation

A Cornish newspaper headline declares: 'Subsidence
fears groundless, insists builder.'

Bill – and coo!

A Croydon reader sends me this notice from a hotel
bedroom in Helsinki: 'In the hotel restaurant the
waitress will give you a bill and you may sign her on the
back side.'

*I have before me a tattered note found in a Berkhamsted
street. It reads: 'Mr Milkman, please could we have 2
extra bottles today only. If this note has blown away,
please knock.'*

Confident type

'Your typing is very neat,' a City office manager was
heard to tell a young agency typist, 'but you should use

the dictionary in the outer office any time you're in doubt about your spelling.' She replied: 'That wouldn't work. I'm never in any doubt.'

School of realism
An artist specialising in marine paintings of storms at sea had some of his work exhibited at St Ives. A schoolgirl who studied the paintings and was then introduced to the artist exclaimed with deep sympathy: 'You really do have terrible luck with the weather!'

Final word
A little while ago the Oxford *Mail* interviewed a man who sells nuclear bomb shelters and mentioned criticism of his company's claim of assuring survival. He replied: 'My comments on this would be to say to the people concerned, if you are not satisfied after a nuclear attack, then you may have a justified complaint.'

A selection of bestsellers from **SPHERE**

FICTION

MANDARIN	Robert Elegant	£2.95 ☐
POSSESSIONS	Judith Michael	£3.95 ☐
KING OF HEAVEN	Burt Hirschfeld	£1.95 ☐
MAN OF WAR	John Masters	£2.50 ☐
FIREFOX DOWN	Craig Thomas	£2.25 ☐

FILM & TV TIE-INS

INDIANA JONES AND THE GIANTS OF THE SILVER TOWER	R. L. Stine	£1.25 ☐
INDIANA JONES AND THE EYE OF THE FATES	Richard Wenk	£1.25 ☐
MINDER – BACK AGAIN	Anthony Masters	£1.50 ☐
SUPERGIRL	Norma Fox Mazer	£1.75 ☐

NON-FICTION

THE FASTEST DIET	Rosie Boycott	£1.25 ☐
THE HYPOCHONDRIAC'S HANDBOOK	Doctors Lee Schreiner and George Thomas	£1.50 ☐
THE ULTIMATE COCKTAIL BOOK	M. C. Martin	£1.95 ☐

All Sphere books are available at your local bookshop or newsagent, or can be ordered direct from the publisher. Just tick the titles you want and fill in the form below.

Name_____

Address_____

_____

Write to Sphere Books, Cash Sales Department, P.O. Box 11, Falmouth, Cornwall TR10 9EN
Please enclose a cheque or postal order to the value of the cover price plus:
UK: 45p for the first book, 20p for the second book and 14p per copy for each additional book ordered to a maximum charge of £1.63.
OVERSEAS: 75p for the first book plus 21p per copy for each additional book.
BFPO & EIRE: 45p for the first book, 20p for the second book plus 14p per copy for the next 7 books, thereafter 8p per book.

Sphere Books reserve the right to show new retail prices on covers which may differ from those previously advertised in the text or elsewhere, and to increase postal rates in accordance with the PO.